Pio Life

by Jan Jorgensen
illustrated by Mark Weber

Harcourt
SCHOOL PUBLISHERS

Requests for permission to make copies of any part of the work should be addressed to School Permissions and Copyrights, Harcourt, Inc., 6277 Sea Harbor Drive, Orlando, Florida 32887-6777. Fax: 407-345-2418.

HARCOURT and the Harcourt Logo are trademarks of Harcourt, Inc., registered in the United States of America and/or other jurisdictions.

Printed in China

ISBN 10: 0-15-350159-6
ISBN 13: 978-0-15-350159-3

Ordering Options
ISBN 10: 0-15-349939-7 (Grade 4 ELL Collection)
ISBN 13: 978-0-15-349939-5 (Grade 4 ELL Collection)
ISBN 10: 0-15-357276-0 (package of 5)
ISBN 13: 978-0-15-357276-0 (package of 5)

5 6 7 8 9 10 0940 12 11 10 09

In the 1800s, many Americans moved west. These people were called pioneers. Pioneers wanted to start new lives. Pioneers wanted to own their own land. They wanted to have their own farms. Pioneers could do this out west. The western part of the United States had a lot of land.

Moving west was difficult. Many people made the long trip in covered wagons. The people faced many dangers. People had to work very hard when they got to their land in the west.

Pioneers had a hard time traveling on land. There were very few roads. The roads were usually old trails that Native Americans had made. The roads were often too skinny for a wagon. Also, roads did not have bridges. It was difficult to cross rivers and streams. Sometimes pioneer wagons got stuck in thick mud.

It was also dangerous to travel through prairies. Prairies are areas where there are few trees. The prairie grass was sometimes taller than an adult. Pioneers often got lost in this tall grass.

Pioneers had to choose where to live. Some pioneer families made their homes near rivers. It was good to live near a river. Pioneers could use the river for transportation. That means that they could travel up and down the river on a raft. Traveling on water was easier than traveling on land. The river also gave pioneers water. They needed water for drinking, cooking, and cleaning. They also needed water for the crops they grew.

Some pioneer families made their homes near thick forests. Pioneers needed the wood that came from the trees. Pioneers used wood to build homes and furniture. Pioneers burned wood to stay warm. They also burned wood to cook their food. The forests had many animals. Pioneers often hunted animals for food. Pioneers who lived close to a forest did not have to go very far to hunt for food.

Most pioneers lived in log cabins. These we small houses made from trees. It took several weeks for a pioneer family to build the log cabin. All the family members helped.

First, they would cut down trees. Then, they would move the logs from the trees to where the cabin would be built. Next, the logs were stacked one on top of another to make walls. The cracks in between the logs were filled in with mud or small pieces of wood. The roofs were made of bark or sod. Sod is a thick section of grass cut from the ground. The floors of log cabins were usually just dirt.

Log cabins had windows, but the windows were not made of glass. Sometimes the windows were covered with animal skins. The animal skins helped to keep out cold air, rain, and snow. Sometimes shutters were placed over the windows. Shutters were thin, wooden boards that could be opened and closed.

Log cabins had fireplaces. The fireplace was where the family burned wood to produce heat or cook food. Most fireplaces were made of rocks. Pioneers often sat close to the fireplace to stay warm on cold nights.

Pioneers had to work hard to get the food they needed. One of the first things pioneer families did was to plant a garden. Pioneers searched the woods for food to eat while waiting for their own plants to grow. Pioneers would look for strawberries and nuts. People also ate green plants, such as dandelions.

Pioneers had vegetables to eat once the plants in the garden grew. People often grew potatoes and turnips. An important crop was corn, which was used to make corn bread and other things.

Pioneers also got food from animals. The pioneers hunted and trapped different wild animals. They ate the meat of bears, deer, and turkeys. Pioneers hunted and ate smaller animals like squirrels. Birds like chickens and quail were food, too.

Many pioneers had their own animals. Families usually had a cow. The cow gave them milk. The milk was used to make cheese and butter.

Pioneers spent most of their time working. There were many things to do. Pioneers had to chop wood to burn in the fire. They had to grow plants and hunt animals. Pioneers had to take care of their animals.

Pioneer women made much of the family's clothing. They even made the shoes. Pioneer men built furniture, such as chairs and beds. Most pioneer children did not go to school. They stayed at the cabin and worked with the family.

Life was difficult for most pioneer families. The pioneers faced many challenges. One challenge they faced was the weather. It was often very cold and snowy in the winter. Heavy snow could trap pioneers in their cabins. Summers could get very hot. Thunderstorms brought dangerous lightning. The lightning sometimes started fires.

Pioneers also had to deal with wild animals. The forests had many animals. Many of the wild animals were dangerous. Pioneers had to protect themselves from large bears. Pioneers also faced dangerous panthers, or mountain lions. Pioneers had to protect their cows, sheep, and pigs from wolves. Wolves would attack and kill these farm animals.

Insects also bothered pioneers. Mosquitoes often stung pioneers. The mosquitoes made many pioneers sick. Some of the mosquitoes carried germs. The pioneers would get a fever. The pioneers would not be able to get out of bed. Pioneers lived deep in the wilderness. There were no doctors close by.

Life for pioneers was very hard, but owning their own land was important to them. It was important enough that they risked their lives to get to their new home. It was important enough that the pioneers were willing to work hard to stay in their new home.

Scaffolded Language Development

CONCEPT REVIEW Talk with students about the pioneers who moved west in the 1800s. Remind students that these people worked hard in order to start a new life. Then have students complete the sentence starters below based on what they read in the book.

1. One reason people moved west was _____.
2. The hardest part of being a pioneer was _____.
3. Pioneers built their cabins out of _____.

Have students say whether they would or would not have wanted to be a pioneer, and why.

 ## Social Studies

Compare and Contrast Have students draw two pictures: one that shows how pioneers lived and one that shows how people live today. Have students write captions for their pictures that point out some of the differences.

School-Home Connection
Pioneer Life Ask students to discuss this story with a family member. Tell them to ask family members whether they have ever moved to a new place and what it was like.

Word Count: 949